sleep

true love

FRIENDSHIP

faith

SYMBOLS

HEALING

REFLECTION

POWER

FORTUNE

DREAMS

Douglas Clucas

Bath New York Singapore Hong Kong Cologne Delhi Melbourne

CONTENTS

This edition published in 2009
Parragon
Queen Street House
4 Queen Street
Bath BA1 1HE, UK

CONCEIVED AND PRODUCED BY Focus
Publishing, Sevenoaks, Kent

PROJECT EDITOR Guy Croton

DESIGNER Philip Clucas MCSD

INDEXER Caroline Watson

ISBN 978-1-4075-6565-1

Printed in China

THE WORLD OF DREAMS

We sleep to revive our bodies and minds. Each night, our sleep patterns progress through different phases of increasingly deeper sleep. This process begins with light sleep when our bodies first relax, and culminates in deep sleep—but it is during the periods of milder sleep that dreaming is likely to occur because our minds are still fairly active. Dreams represent the "spin" our psyche puts upon our emotional desires and fears, rather than a direct portrayal of our waking lives. As the entries below show, there are ten separate categories that dreams fall into.

Psychological healing dreams Although these dreams can be disturbing at times, they are different from nightmares because they represent real situations we may find ourselves in during our daily lives. Often these dreams occur at times of stress or when we have important decisions to make. These dreams should not be viewed negatively, as they often help us heal ourselves and free us from negative emotions.

Belief dreams Dreams have played a part in shaping all major world religions. From Jacob's dreams of angels ascending to heaven, to Mohammed's visionary inspiration for his spiritual mission, dreamlore has been vital to shaping the course, not just of our religious beliefs, but also of world history. Because of their importance, mankind has always been fascinated by dreams and has dedicated much time to trying to understand and analyze them. Because of this, every culture (*top right*) has its own beliefs surrounding dreamscapes.

Problem-solving dreams These dreams usually include a "guide" who imparts an important message to the sleeper which may help them to solve a problem in their waking life—the guide's identity is also paramount.

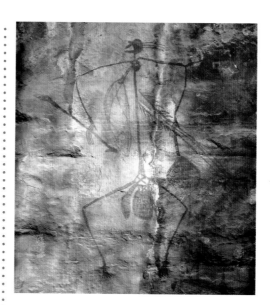

above This 15,000-year-old cave painting is thought to represent a sorcerer assuming the form of a stag. By imagining their quarry in dreams, the tribal Shaman supposedly gained dominion over their prey.

Be led Spiritual guides may take the form of a friend, stranger, or even an animal. If the dreamer finds themself lost at sea, they may be guided to shore by a dolphin. Occasionally animals may speak to the sleeper and offer pertinent advice.

above Images of childhood are common in our dreams because they represent a carefree time when we were protected and loved unconditionally. Such psychological dreams represent a desire for comfort or stability.

Physiological dreams   Some dreams are merely a direct representation of our emotional, psychological, or physical desires. To dream that you are thirsty may simply express the fact that your body craves extra fluid, or to dream that you are walking over a frozen lake might reflect your need for an extra blanket to warm

the bed. This can be carried into our emotions, where the conscious and subconscious become intermixed and entangled.

Dreams of daily life   Dreams of familiar faces, places and events can feel important—precisely because they seem so real. However, they are often among the least instructive of dreams because they are simple echoes of the waking world reflected in our sleep. Such dreams can also be inspired by real disturbances; for example the muffled sound of traffic outside a window can instigate dreams of driving.

Compensatory dreams   Some dreams allow us to do things we would never contemplate in waking life, while others reveal the "shadowed" sides of our personality. Shy people may experience flamboyant images of themselves, whilst those who are usually sexually restrained might dream that they are ravenously promiscuous. Such dreams are designed to balance our personality and give vent to emotions we would not usually seek to experience.

Recurring dreams   Dreams that repeat themselves are a sign of troubles that remain unsolved in our waking lives. Our psyche uses sleep to remind us of the anxieties we feel, the problems we have to resolve and the stresses and strains we are under. These feelings can be expressed in a myriad different ways, though occasionally when the mind discovers a particularly effective method of highlighting such tensions, it will repeat it until the issues that are troubling the dreamer are resolved.

Lucid dreams   In these dreams, the sleeper often knows that they are dreaming. The dream will feel real, but events or characters will be greatly exaggerated. The sleeper will often manipulate these dreams to their own advantage—thus such dreams can be a positive tool to explore new vistas and help resolve conflict.

Premonition/clairvoyant dreams Most people will have experienced visions in their dreams that later appeared to come true. However, rather than displaying any clairvoyant skills, such dreams are common and have a more rational explanation. During our waking lives, our brains absorb a huge amount of information, both consciously and subconsciously; this includes various prompts about the likely behavior of others, especially those we are close to. When people or events unfold as we have "foreseen," we believe them to be prophetic but in fact they are merely the logical unfolding of events that our subconscious has already deduced.

Nightmares Nightmares are the most emotionally draining of all dreams and will be discussed in greater detail later in the book. They

below The Romans thought that dreams held valuable secrets, and temples featured rooms where couples could pay to sleep in the hope of revelation.

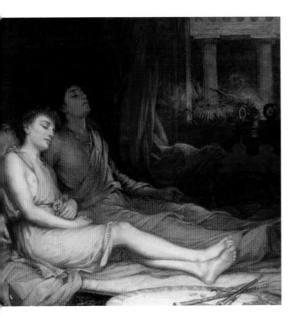

represent concerns in our waking lives which the subconscious mind seeks to emphasize by snaring our attention through fear. Although our dreams can never physically harm us —and even seemingly terrifying dreams are sent to help us—persistent nightmares can be draining if they occur regularly, so confide them to a friend or even a professional counselor.

above Nightmares used to be seen as the work of demons where an "incubus" would sit on the sleeper's chest, inflicting the dreamer with disturbing visions. Understanding nightmares though can actually help instead of hinder your quality of life.

Dreaming allows us to prepare ourselves for the stresses and strains of everyday life as well as the physical challenges.

INSPIRATION AND ANALYSTS

below right *The Shakespeare Window in London's Southwark Cathedral—the Bard's works are scattered with allusions to sleep and the world of the dreamscape.*

Many musicians, artists, writers, and inventors claim to have received inspiration through their dreams. Our minds absorb a great deal of everyday information, both consciously and subconsciously, and the sleeping mind can often sift through this information more effectively when the body is at rest. Although some of these ideas are too bizarre or extreme to be of any use, occasionally the sleeping mind interacts with a fertile imagination to inspire ideas which would never have surfaced during our waking life.

Perhaps the most profound work to be inspired by lucid dreaming was *Alice in Wonderland* by the mathematician Charles Lutwidge Dodgson (Lewis Carroll). Within its pages he successfully amalgamates the surreal elements of dreaming to create a book, not just about a dream, but about dreaming itself. Similarly, Mary Shelley claimed that the inspiration for her book *Frankenstein* was a dream she had after a conversation about the supernatural with her brother Percy Bysshe Shelley and Lord Byron. Unlike Lewis Carroll's approach, her idea was fully formed and based directly upon the images she had envisioned in her dream—rather than the illusive and contradictory nature of dreaming itself.

The Spanish painter Salvador Dalí once claimed his work was a portrayal of reality seen through the subconscious rather than conscious mind, and thus he encapsulates the main elements of dreamlore in his paintings —depicting a land both distortedly surreal, yet hauntingly familiar.

William Shakespeare often refers both directly and indirectly to dreams in his work and the influence they have upon his characters. *A Midsummer Night's Dream* is both a play about dreaming and an analogy of dreaming itself, depicting the confusion that can be caused during sleep. Some people also speculate that the pivotal scene in *Hamlet*—between

the eponymous hero and his father—is in fact a dream, and is the Bard's warning to us never to take dreams at face value.

The great dream analysts

Current understanding suggests that dreams represent our memories—both conscious events we can recall and the subconscious images our brains absorb throughout our waking lives. We may think that the images

we dream about are completely abstract but this is seldom, if ever, the case. They may be inspired by conversations we have overheard but not consciously registered or images that have passed by so quickly that our cognizant minds fail to "apprehend" them. Whatever the case, it is the emotion that such fragments trigger that are vital to the understanding of the dreamscape.

Sigmund Freud is the best known of the great dream analysts. He stressed the crucial role of the subconscious in the shaping of our dreams, noting that dreams work on two levels—the "manifest" or conscious, and the "latent" or subconscious level. Dreams of sexual desire or violent intent are expressed in the subconscious, free from personal or social taboos, and represent wish fulfillment.

Alfred Adler introduced the theory of "individual psychology" which stresses the importance of one's desires upon their dreams —for example, feelings of inadequacy in childhood will later be replaced by dreams of empowerment in adult life.

Carl Jung introduced the idea of the "collective unconscious." He believed that there was a universal symbolic language which could be used to explain anyone's individual dreams, regardless of their culture, religion, or beliefs.

The pages that follow

The following pages present a collection of the most commonly encountered symbols that constitute the language of dreams. They can help to explain more about your psyche.

above right *Carl Jung's work led to a closer evaluation of the universal symbolism featured in dreams, rather than placing all the emphasis on the individual's personality.*

above left *Sigmund Freud believed that imagery featured in sexual dreams were littered with phallic symbolism such as rearing serpents, guns, and keys.*

FAMILIAR FEATURES

Where we live and what we eat are important to us all. They are the foundations of life which offer comfort and security, helping us raise our families and grow. It is hardly surprising therefore that each play such a prominent role in dreamlore. Turning first to where we live, houses have often been linked symbolically with the womb, representing a cocoon which no external force can penetrate. In dreams, home is the place we go in times of insecurity and uncertainty—a shelter from all that threatens to overwhelm us, and to dream of one's home is a positive and healthy sign.

The home of your dreams

Everyone has their own individual ideas of their dream home. For some it may be in the heart of a city, for others it could be the back of beyond. These wishes hold special resonance in dreams and tell us as much about ourselves as people as they do about our home-loving aspirations.

A country cottage may represent a desire to escape the worries and monotony of everyday life, and substitute the rat-race for a more leisurely existence.

Dreams of a childhood home generally display a longing for a return to an easier way of life; it is likely that you are facing several problems in your current life and your subconscious is yearning for a return to a simpler time.

Crossing the threshold

It is not merely the type or positioning of a home that is important in dreamlore; all elements of the house have their own resonance.

The front door represents one's passage between particular states of mind or beliefs. If a door is seen to be locked or bolted, it represents a barrier through which only those with a key may pass. Keys can symbolize the ability to unlock, or unpick, problems. Whoever is seen in a dream

opposite page *A home in the country can represent the desire for a simpler way of life and a place to establish a solid family base for you and your loved ones. But be wary of closed gates—these can represent that the dreamer is guarded.*

above *A lush garden not only looks beautiful but also reflects the dreamer's personality as someone who is prepared to go the distance and be patient in achieving their goals. Those who dream of vast gardens are likely to be more restless.*

Familiar Features

below *Dreams of our family home on fire may be representative of the anger we are suppressing when we are awake, and the acknowledgement that these emotions have the power to destroy that which we hold most dear.*

holding a key may also hold the answer to any dilemma the dreamer is currently struggling with. If the dreamer holds the key themself, it suggests that given time and patience, they can resolve their own problems.

The home dreamscape

Different rooms in the house hold different connotations in dreamlore. At the top of the house, the attic symbolizes intellect and curiosity. Bedrooms characteristically represent security and rest, though they can also hold sexual connotations. For example, small or cramped bedrooms may signify illicit feelings and secret desires.

Bathrooms in the dreamscape are synonymous with purification and the washing away of past indiscretions. Dirty washing water

foretells the shame of an unworthy act. Living rooms or dining areas symbolize our personal relations with others. If someone else is in the room, their manner toward you is important. If they are hostile, it suggests that you will experience problems with a lover or friend, but if they are welcoming, this may herald the re-establishment of old acquaintances.

Household omens

Even everyday objects can offer a wealth of symbolism. Candles and lamps bring light into the darkness of our homes, and symbolize mankind's desire to illuminate our lives.

Dreaming specifically of a candle can symbolize a spark of inspiration that will deliver insight into a current spiritual dilemma or signpost the direction of possible solutions

where none have previously been thought to exist.

Dreaming of a full cup can indicate that we are positive about our life—and heralds a time of self-created prosperity; however, if the cup is seen to be empty, the omens are reversed. To see a kettle boiling illustrates that current family problems will soon come to an end. If the kettle is worn, it may signify that there will be hard times ahead before things improve.

Empty chairs indicate that patience is needed to achieve a long-held ambition. If the chair is occupied by someone, it may signal that person is currently "standing in your shadow"—this does not mean that you need to cut them out of your life but, on the contrary, it illustrates a need to deal with the problems of others before your own.

left *Gardens are said to emphasize the female aspect of dreams; and nothing better illustrates this than* In a Shoreham Garden *by the visionary artist Samuel Palmer, in which he pays homage to the spirit of Springtide fecundity.*

below *Dreaming of living in a city can represent an innate desire for financial success—but be careful of how you go about achieving such wealth.*

Where you see your ideal home located can reveal much about what motivates you as a person both mentally and spiritually.

FOOD FOR THOUGHT

below The symbolism of food is considered to be fortuitous; however, if we overindulge, the omens associated with food will quickly be reversed—so consider yourself warned!

Not only do we need food and drink to nourish and sustain us, it is also one of our greatest pleasures. Even when awake we sometimes daydream about the foods we love, thus it should come as no surprise that its images infiltrate our sleep.

The type of meal we see ourselves eating can also play a role. Breakfasts talk of a wealth of opportunity that lies invitingly in the dreamer's path; a rushed lunch may imply impatience, and dinner is a meal of many shades. To eat alone forecasts a reassessing of priorities whilst those that share a meal are likely to forge a lasting friendship.

We should not forget that we eat to live, rather than live to eat.

Basic ingredients

Bread represents peace and wellbeing. Kneading dough in a dream shows a confidence in our own abilities, whilst breaking bread with others demonstrates the value that the dreamer places upon the bonds of friendship.

In dreamlore potatoes have come to represent stability in the home, and earthy responses to earthy problems. To see yourself eating this food staple implies reticence, but with a decided lack of imaginative flair.

Meat is considered to represent lust and pent-up emotion—highlighting the "sins of the flesh," in which a loveless sexual encounter may be likened to two dead carcasses joined but devoid of the living soul.

Rice is another staple food of many diets and denotes confidence in business ventures.

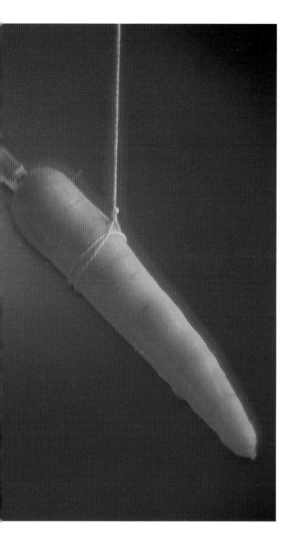

love, rotten cauliflowers signal failure due to a neglect of duty, and moldy onions speak of spite and envy.

While debate surrounds whether a tomato is a vegetable or a fruit, its role in dreamlore is clearer. Picking a tomato forebodes bad luck and libelous gossip, though eating it indicates the recovery of lost esteem.

Forbidden fruit

Fruit holds a wealth of sexual symbolism—cherries are a voluptuous fruit, which in shape resembles our erogenous zones, and in dreams, they hint at a future sexual encounter.

Thanks to Eve's gift to Adam, apples are linked to original sin and in dreamlore, apples still carry their earlier caution against letting ourselves be ruled by our libido.

above *Dreaming of carrots means happiness and good health; a woman dreaming of them could mean the promise of a large family in the future.*

Green cuisine

Dreaming of planting vegetables is a sign of a need for future planning, suggesting that the dreamer should start concentrating on the future rather than the present.

Those who see themselves picking vegetables will soon be rewarded. However, if the vegetables harvested are moldy or rotten, this is a sign that the sleeper's plans are doomed to fail. Indeed each vegetable and its condition has dreamlore significance. Wilted cabbages denote disappointment in

below *Eating a peach in a dream is regarded as a forecasting of good fortune. In China, peaches are considered particularly auspicious, as they are associated with the god of long life, Shou Hsing.*

Familiar Features

above left *To dream of drinking wine or champagne indicates a need for discretion to avoid public criticism. Beer can denote disappointment.*

above right *Dreams of ice cream can mean us reconnecting with our "inner child"—enjoy such dreams, as they presage success in ventures already underway.*

Oranges speak of short but sweet encounters, grapes of a long and affectionate union, and strawberries of true love. Lemons, however, represent bitterness and jealousy, whilst blackberries and raspberries indicate emotional entanglements and infidelity.

Naughty... but nice!

Cakes are representational of "giving." To dream of being handed a piece of cake by another is a sign that you are held in high regard by colleagues and friends. To see oneself sharing a cake with others is indicative of a generous personality and demonstrates the sleeper's tendency not to merely limit their friendship to one person, or a group of people, but to bestow their affections on a wide social circle. Linked to this, pastries denote heartfelt friendships, and cookies indicate a warm and generous persona.

Childhood favorites like ice cream tend to reawaken the "inner child" within us all. Dreaming of eating a bowl of jello or sucking on old-fashioned candies are likely to predict a reunion with a childhood friend—or perhaps even a sweetheart.

Excess!

To dream of attending a bountiful banquet overflowing with lavish foods and drink whilst surrounded by other guests may seem wonderful but the food merely distracts the dreamer from the fact that they are most likely seldom spoken to by any of the guests and they rarely eat anything—so the dream's symbolism may suggest illness or social exclusion.

Eating too much represents a lack of self control. Dreaming that one continually eats but never feels full is a sign that the dreamer is failing to find rewards in their life—it suggests they may need to think about changing to a more rewarding job, or undertaking some form of charity work in order to make a tangible difference to their world.

Sometimes in dreams we are hurt by the foods we crave. We may see ourselves literally "slipping on a banana skin" or eating something that we know to be poisonous—but that we eat anyway! These dreams reflect the danger of eating too much in real life; telling us that although we feel comforted by some foods, they are causing us more harm than good.

Sᴡᴇᴇᴛ Chocolate is believed to represent a desire to make money. Those that dream of eating chocolate enjoy spending their earnings, while those that hoard their treats have a more considered approach to the future.

right Fresh or clear water symbolizes health and the cleansing of the body and spirit. To imagine drinking warm water signifies sickness.

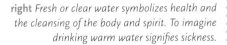

Dreams of alcoholic drinks can be double-edged—whilst seeing oneself enjoying a drink with friends can be a fortuitous sign of social "lubrication," intoxication forebodes disgrace and personal shame.

WORK AND PLAY

Work can fill our lives so it is only natural that it can take up time in our dreamspace as well, but it is vital that we balance punishing deadlines with time to play also—and even dreams of leisurely pursuits can reveal a lot about the state of our lives. Because of society's seeming obsession with careers, this chapter begins though with a profile of how careers affect the dreamscape. For example, it is common for teachers to dream of losing control of a class or for builders to see their constructions collapse. Such dreams are not premonitions, just reminders that one must take time out.

Working "angst"

The pressure of work gets to us all at some point in our lives, and although we might try to hide it externally from others, internally we cannot escape the stresses and strains which end up coloring our dreams.

A common theme may involve visualizing a moving cog. This literally originates from the idea that we are all cogs in one giant wheel (*left*)—our careers!

Dreaming of having too much to do and too little time in which to do it is a sign that you are struggling to organize your time properly. In such cases, it is advisable to spend a little time planning your schedule.

Fear of losing your job symbolizes how important your career is to you, but ironically augurs well for the future, hinting at success and possible promotion.

Workplace symbolism

Many spend so long at work that it is only natural that the images we absorb during the day find their way into our dreams. However, these objects are often more than mere reflections of our daily lives and each possess their own unique symbolism. In dreamlore the office rarely represents business matters.

above *The slog of work can sometimes be seen in dreams in the form of taking to the track as an athlete—and running and running. Time to take a vacation…*

Our careers can consume our dream lives as well as our real lives.

Work and Play

right *Dreaming of attending a "make-or-break" meeting (invariably while battling against the clock) suggests that the sleeper has an important and timely decision to make in their waking life—the outcome of which could affect many more people than just themselves.*

Usually dreams are more closely linked to the sleeper's personal and romantic life than to the sleeper's actual career.

Dreaming of working in an office (even if you do not normally do so in your daily life) indicates that you have been neglecting those who you love, and need to show them more warmth and affection. Visualizing yourself in someone else's office, with or without their permission to be there, suggests strong bonds of affection toward that person. However, for the sleeper to visualize themself relocating to a new workplace could indicate a split with an old friend or the breakdown of a current relationship.

In a dream, the unconscious mind utilizes any object from which it feels able to derive symbolism. Thus items inside an office or studio each invite interpretation. An untidy desk covered in papers indicates hurried decisions that may cost the dreamer dearly. Computers symbolize logic and order, and an inability to use them in a dream signifies that the sleeper may feel uncomfortable with technology, or that a particular project seems overwhelming.

There are many metaphors associated with the workplace, but one that infiltrates our dreams more than most is the image of climbing the career ladder. It is a sign that we are striving to achieve our ambitions, whether they be in business or other areas of our lives.

Too late Punctuality can play on the minds of dreamers who need to make a critical decision in their waking life.

right *Dreaming of a golden nest egg heralds the arrival of an unexpected piece of good news, or the sudden recovery from illness.*

Money matters!

To dream of being short of money denotes the sleeper's fears of illness and death, or negative feelings associated with self-worth. Finding money is a surprisingly common dream that promises future good fortune—however this largesse must be spent wisely or the omens are reversed and the lucky dream recipient will fail to make the most of the opportunities granted to them.

To dream of investing your money wisely suggests a methodical (some might say "plodding") mind, whereas to imagine hoarding large amounts of money unnecessarily in a dream warns the dreamer against fostering an uncharitable and darkened heart.

The illusion of riches

Dreaming of winning a lottery or suddenly acquiring vast wealth may seem fortuitous, but is usually interpreted as an ill omen. Such dreams generally denote loss whilst, paradoxically, to dream of giving away large sums signifies that the dreamer will enjoy a secure financial future.

Visions of living the high life may represent wish fulfillment for many, but to see these visions recurring in sleep is usually a rejoinder from the psyche to set our priorities in order —to realize that "we are who we are" and live to our own potential, not bask in the vacuous envy of others.

Images we often associate with the rich and famous seldom hold positive connotations in dreamlore. For instance, large stately homes and mansions may seem ideal and the perfect place to spend your days not working, but hold omens that imply unforeseen misfortune in the midst of idyllic contentment.

right Dreaming of coins is considered to be good luck. To dream of having a bag or pocket of coins speaks of rapid advancement along a chosen career path.

LEISURE PURSUITS

right and below
Dreaming of taking part in sports, whether they be as diverse as boxing or jousting, is not merely about the winning or the losing—it's about how you take part in the event and how you conduct yourself in a competitive environment.

While individual sports and leisure pursuits each contain their own symbolism, if we regularly dream about taking part in any sporting activity or expressing our artistic skills, we are being encouraged to make changes to our lives. This could simply mean becoming more physically active, or making the most of the talents we are lucky enough to possess; or it may be that we need to sit down and seriously reassess the way we spend our waking lives and set aside more time for the activities that actually make us happy.

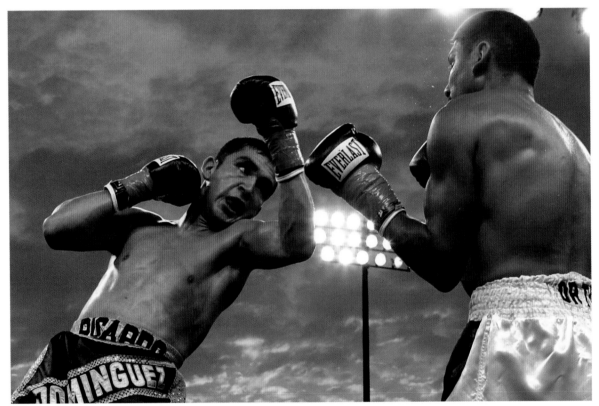

What price victory?

In the dreamscape, images of winning are highly emotive and can fill us with an enormous amount of pride and self-satisfaction, yet in our dreams, as in real life, it is not the victory that is truly important but the manner in which it was achieved. To visualize winning a hard-fought contest can feel personally satisfying. These dreams reflect the bravery and dedication we need to display in our waking lives—to find a "cause" worthy enough. For others, dreaming of a hard-earned "victory against the odds" could imply that the sleeper has abilities that have previously been suppressed but may, if they believed in themself enough, be released to help achieve goals considered impossible.

left *Dreaming of running can be either liberating or excruciatingly painful. Jogging represents the dreamer's desire to achieve a personal ambition.*

below *If you are facing a tough choice in your waking life and you dream of winning trophies or medals, this suggests you will make the right decision.*

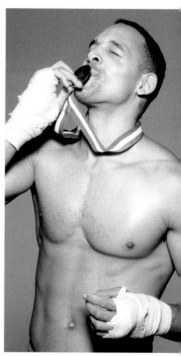

Sporting metaphors

Dreamlore is filled with metaphors of two equals struggling for supremacy, the most obvious being boxing. It has come to represent an internal battle fought within the sleeper—where two conflicting issues remain unresolved. For example, to dream of participating in a fight may represent a clash between the dreamer's public and private persona.

Get active!

Dreaming of exercise is our psyche's less-than-subtle way of telling us we need to "get active"—for our own good. To dream of being able to run at fantastic speeds, or leap incredible distances and never tire, indicates that the sleeper should easily achieve the desired success.

Highs and lows

To see oneself climbing in a dream is a sign of personal ambition. The climb is symbolic of the dreamer striving to "reach higher"—the tougher the ascent, the greater the reward will be. Visions of falling are one of the most disturbing, yet frequently reported themes.

Although vertigo or falling may presage a shattering of the dreamer's ambitions, this sensation of slipping through the air into nothingness is more closely associated with stress, fear, and anxiety in waking life, rather than your imminent demise!

If you dream of bending rules to achieve victory, this implies you need to be careful.

above *Dreaming of challenging exercise in which we may be caked in mud and sweat, represents the dreamer's willingness to push themself to the limits in order to achieve a personal goal—to strive forward with but one ambition, despite the pain!*

Musical instruments hold their own symbolism, and to dream of playing one (even if in waking life you would not know one end of that instrument from the other) suggests that you actually please a loving partner—even though you sometimes doubt it. To imagine playing the piano signifies that you will find a valuable object in the most unlikely place. Guitars suggest a nimbleness and lightness of touch when dealing with difficult situations while saxophones and other brass instruments hold out the prospect that something unexpectedly interesting will happen shortly.

"High rolling"

To dream of gambling and winning can seem ideal—forecasting luck and the tantalizing prospect of future wealth. However, such visions

In dreams, swimming can represent a freedom from social constraint and is the mind's way of releasing tension through dreams. Drowning, however, suggests that the sleeper feels overwhelmed by problems in their life and is finding it hard to cope.

Music in our dreams

Music is usually a positive omen in our dreams. To hear music in your sleep indicates a sense of harmony in your waking life, suggesting equilibrium between social relationships, family concerns, and your career.

Hymns denote contentment, sea shanties a thirst for adventure, operatic melodies a desire to express oneself succinctly—while songs we remember from our youth imply a desire for a less complicated lifestyle.

right *In dreams, swimming is a sensation closely akin to unaided flight—Freud believed there were sexual connotations to the leisure pursuit as well.*

left *Although we may dream of a certain horse winning a race, or believe we see a number or name emerge in our sleep, the images we envision represent a desired outcome of wishful thinking —and seldom, if ever, the correct forecast to a sports event.*

below *To dream of reading indicates a desire to widen one's horizons, and it is important that the sleeper takes note of the details of the book, as this will suggest possible routes to follow. Alternatively, the book may be one which is unwritten and one you should consider writing!*

are just a reflection of the dreamer's desire for "easy money," and if acted upon are more likely to lead to failure than success and prosperity.

The arts

In dreamlore, as in real life, the arts can bring great pleasure. Dreaming of undertaking an artistic pursuit demonstrates the sleeper's subconscious desire to explore their own gifts.

For example, dreams in which the sleeper imagines themselves as an actor or actress may demonstrate that they have a difficult decision to make which has long term repercussions.

The audience's reaction to the dreamer's performance is important—if the dreamer receives applause, it suggests that their decision will meet with widespread approval, whilst if they are booed or are met with a stony silence, the omens are far from perfect, so do step on to that stage with care!

Finally, to dream of learning lines can mean wanting the approval of your peers—to be seen to be "making the right noises" in life generally.

If you dream of watching an opera, remember the genre you saw—it could mirror future prospects in your waking life.

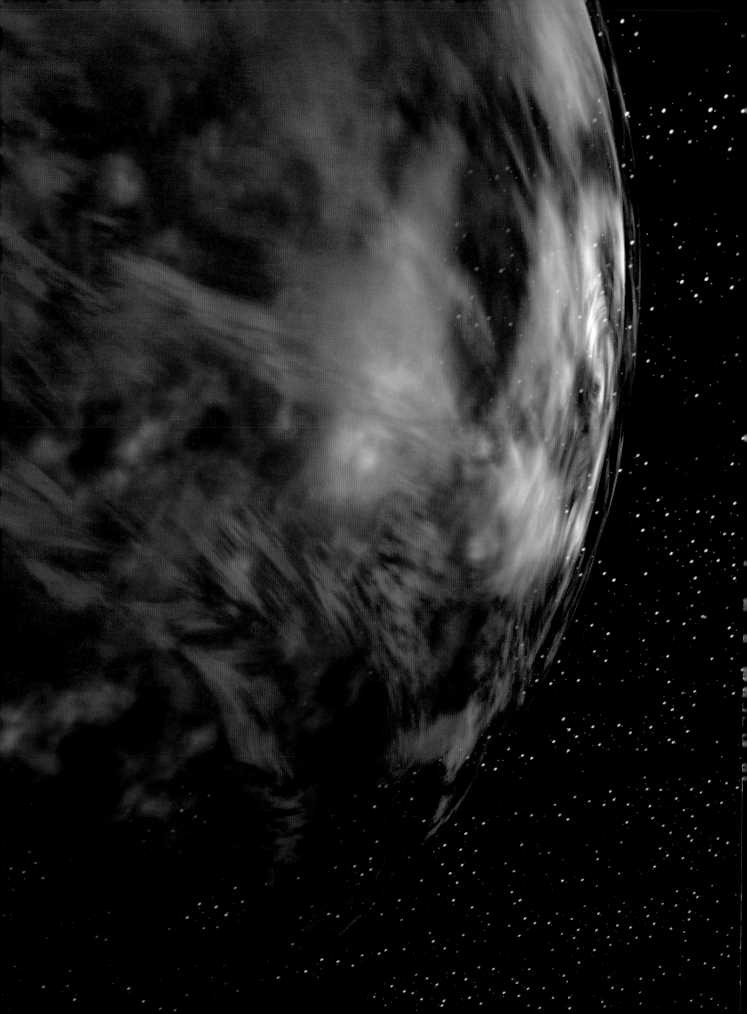

THE JOURNEY

Dreams of travel are not simply a way of urging the sleeper to expand their horizons and make more of themselves. The transport we use for our dream journeys, the paths we travel, and the experiences we encounter along the way are all important to understanding their meaning. Routes are rarely traversed with ease, and obstacles experienced relate to the difficulties faced in waking life. The people we encounter often have echoes in the real world, and arriving at a destination is an auspicious omen —hinting of goals that the sleeper has set for themself.

The road ahead

In dreamlore, roads and paths represent the route to personal ambition. They may be short-term objectives, like promotion at work or getting fit; or longer term ambitions, such as commitment to marriage and raising a family.

Long, straight roads are rare in the dreamscape but if they do appear, they signify that the dreamer will be able to achieve their aims easily if they have the right level of desire and choose to apply the correct level of effort. More common is a winding pathway or rambling country lane, with each bend signifying a possible obstacle or pitfall that must be negotiated.

Forks in the road denote events that could divert you from your chosen path. If the road selected leads to a dead-end, it implies the dreamer has made a wrong choice in their waking life which they may need to re-evaluate. Crossroads hint that the sleeper has reached a stage in life where an important decision must be made.

Over land and sea

The type of transportation that our subconscious mind chooses to utilize in a dream can be significant. In dreamscapes, cycling can be

above Like in life, the path and roads featured in our dreams are rarely perfect and straight—they must be negotiated with care one step at a time to ensure a safe arrival at the other end.

Travel in dreams represents the physical and spiritual.

PAGAN Wheels represent continuation—they are symbolic of the pagan "circle of life," in which each season and component of the year is reflected by one of the wheel's spokes.

right *Lighthouses are dream harbingers of safety; they offer a beacon of light and, as such, illuminate a wise course of action in a sea of uncertainty. It urges the sleeper to listen to their instincts rather than be swayed by popular opinion.*

below right *To travel in a space shuttle reflects a desire for excitement and adventure.*

an outward reflection of the dreamer's view of life—if they are constantly cycling uphill, this is a sign that they view life as a struggle and believe that rewards can only be achieved by hard work.

To view yourself driving an automobile is an affirmative omen and indicates a desire to take control of your own destiny—although to crash or veer out of control indicates you are not as confident as you would like to think.

Trains, when dreamt about, indicate confidence and the belief in a rosy future; though to see a loved one leaving on a train signifies a current emotional distancing between them and yourself.

Ships and boats hark back to mankind's long fascination with the sea and to dream of crossing an ocean in one relates to a long-held desire for independence.

Into the air... and beyond

Dreaming of unaided flight represents a desire to be free from the boundaries that we, or others, daily place upon ourselves. To dream

of piloting a plane is an emphatic statement of self-confidence. It suggests that the dreamer has either discovered a new-found belief in their own ability or they should give themselves greater credit for their recent achievements. To be a passenger on a plane suggests that you will receive good fortune, but through no apparent effort of your own.

Thanks to technology, we are no longer restricted to our own world and can visualize travel to other galaxies. Dreams that explore the depths of space represent our psyche's desire to challenge our own preconceptions.

Classic travel symbolism

Wheels in dreams symbolize home where, like the wheel (that returns to its original position),

we are always destined to return. Steps symbolize success either in social or financial matters. To be seen walking up a flight of stairs is a sign of achievement, whilst to walk down can be taken as a sign of failure or simply the fear of over-stretching one's talents.

A compass expresses a desire for self-improvement—though it is the direction in which the needle points that is the defining factor. East represents dawn and youth, and hints at a need for the dreamer to return to past values. West is symbolic of sunset and rebirth —an omen of change. North is supposedly connected to the soul and speaks of a desire for spiritual enrichment, while finally, the South is warm and exotic and foretells joy in social relationships.

above Maps in dreams denote order and precision. While they may represent travel, they are more commonly linked to an inner desire to reorganize one's own life —to put private affairs in order and to complete tasks that have long lain neglected.

TIME AND SPACE

below *Dreaming of winter means the mind is taking stock of your life and preparing for what the new year will bring.*

Both time and space are human concepts used to explain and compartmentalize the rational world. However, our subconscious needs no such boundaries and can play with these concepts to rationalize the seemingly irrational. Despite this lack of spatial and timely restraint, dreams of time and space have their own rationale which need interpretation.

Dreaming of the time of the day is relatively common, especially the dawn and dusk. Sunrise is representative of a fresh start and new opportunities for those willing to seize them, whilst sunset is the mind's attempt to reflect on past successes and failures.

Dreams of traveling through the infinity of space are also familiar to many sleepers; dreams such as these hint at changing circumstances and widening prospects.

The round of the year

In dreamlore, each season of the year holds its own individual resonance. Spring is the season of reawakening and rebirth and is closely linked to inspiration and the innocence of first love. To dream of a bright spring day foretells new opportunities, especially for romance. Traditionally spring was also a time of departure, and in medieval times became closely linked with pilgrimage. Thus, spring can also represent the renewal of a quest, urging the dreamer to abandon the comfort zone of certainty to encompass new challenges.

The "hazy, lazy, mazy days of summer" are seen in dreamlore to represent the "wine of friendship." If the dreamer envisages themselves relaxing in the sun with others, it suggests strong bonds of friendship, or even love with

In our dreams, days can disappear into mere seconds, while seconds can last an entire lifetime—all because there are no rules in sleep.

one member of the group. Fall, meanwhile, is the time of harvest and in dreamlore this tells the sleeper to reap the rewards of that which they have sown, for unless success is celebrated, it is destined to wither on the vine.

Winter has been associated with death in the past but in dreamlore, it is a period of contemplation rather than despair.

Worlds beyond

The question of whether we are alone in the universe is one that continues to fascinate mankind. Whatever the truth, we know that there are millions of planets in the universe other than our own.

Dreaming of stars usually represents the sleeper's wish to control their fate—a single star appearing brighter than others represents a particularly auspicious development in the near future for the slumbering dreamer.

The moon represents our emotions and quest for self-improvement. Its wandering across the night sky reflects the shifting pattern of our own lives.

above Dreaming of stars or of traveling through space is normally an indicator of a desire for control and the expansion of one's horizons.

THE NATURAL WORLD

From the highest mountain to the smallest stream, from the incredible force of a volcano to the earth's natural treasures such as gems and gold, dreams of the natural world serve to remind us of nature's beauty and power. However, dreams focusing on such earthy elements emphasize parts of our lives by illustrating our current physical, spiritual, or emotional wellbeing. For example, mountains represent achievement and a desire to strive toward success while water is strongly linked to our emotions. Views of gently rolling hills and fields (*left*) evoke a sense of wellbeing.

Lush forests and arid wastes

Dreams of forests and woods have come to represent feelings of unease with one's life. To imagine being lost in a forest denotes that the sleeper feels overcome by the pressures of everyday life; this is usually closely linked to financial matters, but can also represent feelings of social isolation or perhaps a lack of personal direction.

These dreams can be further complicated by the appearance of thorns and briars which conspire to ensnare the sleeper, preventing a move forward. A forest fire may further endanger the dream traveler within the landscape, and underlines the powerful message the subconscious seeks to deliver.

"Through hollow lands and hilly lands..."

Dreaming of mountains symbolizes aspiration and the search for higher meaning. For those that stand at its foot, a mountain represents obstacles to be conquered.

Similarly, mountains denote troubles in the dreamer's life that they may feel are difficult to overcome, or a task that appears almost impossible. However daunting it may appear, the dreamer will usually find that if they start their climb, it is not as hard as they expected. While

DESTRUCTION Dreams of destroying the landscape are symbolic of our own self-destructive sides; are we denying our true emotions in our waking life?

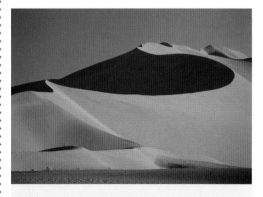

BARREN The arid waste of the desert has come to symbolize troubled times in the dreamer's life, and their need to rely on others to help them through.

The Natural World

SAND IN HAND Wet sand upon our skin can be an irritant and reminds us not to be complacent in our lives and embrace all we have gratefully.

above *Jungles and rainforests hold similar connotations to forests, although they have the added dangers of deadly animals and poisonous plants.*

mountains represent the ferocity of the elements and the unconquerable power of nature, valleys are seen as welcoming and habitable. To dream of a fertile valley with an abundance of flora and fauna foretells successful parenthood, while barren valleys imply family troubles. A valley shrouded in darkness or engulfed by mist indicates problems in a relationship.

Rivers, lakes, and streams

In dreamlore, flowing water symbolizes our life-force. Clear, swift currents indicate health and success, while shallow, brackish water heralds possible stagnation and indecision.

Lakes indicate our mood. A placid surface unfurrowed by ripples and movement suggests contentment with life, while stormy waters denote that the dreamer is troubled by negative emotions. To see moonlight reflected in the surface of a lake suggests the sleeper is becoming emotionally involved with a partner who shares their intensity of feeling.

To see a small stream in a dream can represent creativity. To bathe in the waters is a sign of a desire—to embrace your talent and to use it to your full advantage. However, an unwillingness to submerge may illustrate that the dreamer is reluctant to use their creative skills to full capacity.

Rivers represent the dreamer's lifespan. Fast-flowing water suggests a carefree attitude to life and a desire to embrace all it has to offer; while a meandering river full of bends implies the dreamer is plodding through life with little direction and even less enthusiasm. To dream of crossing a river is an indication that the sleeper has a decision to make; the degree of difficulty experienced in crossing will serve to indicate how hard this choice will be.

right *Mountains in dreams should not simply be seen as merely negative—to reach the summit is a positive sign of advancement; one of social or spiritual maturity.*

The Natural World

The seas and wide ocean

Calm seas are a sign of inner peace and contentment while stormy oceans represent troubled times ahead. Any dreams of the ocean can be linked to feelings of love, though rarely are they positive. Dreaming of crossing an ocean may represent a romantic challenge, although the progress and condition of the vessel you envisage to complete the ocean crossing is important—if it flounders, this is a discouraging omen... worse still if it sinks!

Despite such negative omens, many dreams of the sea may be viewed as life affirming. To dream of wading in a clear blue ocean signifies confidence in your own ability; swimming in the sea is a sign of "washing away" your worries; while dreaming of diving in illustrates a wonderfully relaxed spirit.

above *To dream that one is underwater floating over a reef is a form of pure escapism. Be wary though—such dreams could mean you are unable to face real situations and there is a real need to tackle issues in our waking lives.*

To dream of a desert island may seem idyllic, but can represent a sense of boredom in the dreamer's realm.

The Natural World

ELEMENTAL FORCES

The power of nature can be both wonderful and terrifying. In dreams elemental forces play a pivotal role, often directly mirroring the power of nature with extremes of emotions.

Weather lore

In dreamlore rain is a lucky omen. To dream of being caught out in the rain is considered a sign of joyous fortune. A gentle shower symbolizes good grace and improved luck.

Rime—frozen water vapor upon winter trees—sits uneasily upon the dreamscape, where it forewarns the sleeper not to claim success for a venture until the rewards have safely been achieved. Similarly, frost warns against promises that can easily be broken, though the appearance of icicles implies that you are in danger of appearing emotionally cold.

Mist and fog are usually a sign that the dreamer is trying to conceal something in their waking life. Often this is a guilty secret kept from others, but may also represent the sleeper's waking mind attempting to hide their own true feelings from themselves.

The four elements

The four elements of Water, Air, Fire, and Earth have great potency and importance within the world of dreamlore.

In dreams, water is commonly regarded as a precursor of good fortune, although there are notable exceptions—spilling water denotes a quarrel, and to view one's reflection warns against placing too much gravitas upon one's own opinions.

To dream of warm air cautions against the possible onset of a self-inflicted illness, whilst to imagine cold air blowing against the body suggests a reflection upon the suitability of a current tryst.

To dream of fire is an indication that the sleeper is presently ruled by their emotions and might benefit from a greater degree of self-

above *Natural disasters such as volcanoes cause devastation and such catastrophes in our waking lives evoke uncomfortable symbolism in our dreams.*

WINDY To imagine that a wind blows in a dream often enhances the highly surreal nature of the dreamscape, adding an element of unease—the greater the wind's force, the more potent the symbolic omens are considered to be.

Earthquakes are seen to be linked to upheaval in our personal lives.

control. Earth is a practical element that when viewed in dreams implies a rise in status—from a position of scorn to one of honor.

The raging earth

The absolute power of nature should never be underestimated. In dreams, tidal waves represent strong emotions that threaten to "sweep you off your feet." Drought is an omen of misfortune and it may signify that you are putting a lot of effort into a venture which will produce little reward; such dreams though can prepare you for similar pitfalls in the future.

Although floods can be very destructive, in dreams they can be positive and have come to represent the end of an old way of life and the beginning of a new one.

below *Smoldering volcanoes in dreams represent the repression of emotions that threaten to "explode." Often this pent-up passion is linked with unfulfilled carnal desires, but this frustration can just as easily represent jealousy or envy. These feelings should be addressed during waking hours, so as not to consume us.*

EARTHLY TREASURES

Dreaming of precious stones and metallic treasures is often believed to foretell financial reward; however, this is seldom the case. In fact, the more earthly treasures you accumulate in a dream generally implies the less your materialistic gain is likely to be. Those who dream of finding treasure may discover improvements in their social life or romantic prospects, rather than in their bank balance. Although this apparent reversal of fortune may disappoint some dreamers, it should be remembered that wealth is transient, whereas emotional riches, health, and contentment far outweigh financial reward.

Adding sparkle to sleep

Dreaming of finding any precious stone is a positive sign. Like fairytales we may sometimes envisage treasure being guarded by dragons or other mythical beasts; this symbolism is conjured up by the subconscious mind to illustrate, not merely the importance we place upon such riches, but also the subliminal feelings that treasures should be earned by hard graft rather than simply taken when stumbled upon. However, rarely do riches in dreams signify material wealth; more often they denote physical or spiritual quests and attainments.

Of all the precious stones, diamonds are the most valued and sought after. They are the hardest of any known substance and can only be cut by themselves—thus diamonds symbolize permanence and incorruptibility.

Other precious stones are closely linked to our emotions. Rubies—greatly revered in the Middle Ages as a cure-all for plague and poisoning—denote passion and the enslavement of desire. Sapphires, with their shimmering blue tint, embody the virtues of resilience and truth.

Emeralds, once believed to be the solidified form of serpent venom, have a poisonous portent for those who dream of the green jewel—said to induce envy in those who view it in sleep. Amethysts, topaz, and lapis lazuli all warn the dreamer to beware the dangers of intoxication, unchecked desire, and pride respectively.

Gems are most commonly seen during dreams, as in waking life, as adornments—necklaces foretell the accumulation of wealth, bracelets indicate the spread of gossip about you, whilst for an unfortunate sailor to dream of an earring supposedly forecasts a watery death by drowning.

Precious metals

Generally dreams of metal represent the sleeper's "cold" or "hard" qualities and suggest they would benefit from a more relaxed approach to life; however, specific metals also have their own individual meanings. In dreamlore gold is closely associated with honor and success—it delivers the "shining prizes." Silver is said to act as a warning against the shortcoming of others, especially untrustworthy friends.

above Pearl represents hidden beauty and to dream of one means that love may be found in the unlikeliest of places.

far right The beauty of the earth is shown in the gems it produces. These jewels are highly prized treasures.

The appearance of amber in dreams denotes balance, inner wisdom, and harmony within the sleeper.

below *Those who dream of ivory should be wary of easy wealth attained through investing in risky ventures.*

above *Eons ago, gold was seen as the encapsulation of the power of the sun in solidified form. Because it won't rust, it was regarded as pure and incorruptible.*

Copper objects signify unfounded worries, brass represents emotional strength, zinc indicates substantial and energetic progress, and lead warns against lethargy and placing too much reliance upon the goodwill of others. Iron appears in dreams as a sign denoting personal success and empowerment; however, if rust is seen on a surface it denotes romantic problems, while to get the metallic stain upon your fingers indicates failure of a cherished goal.

ANIMALS AND PLANTS

Animals and plants can figure large in our waking lives, so it is only natural that they feature in our dreamscape. From time immemorial animals and plants have delighted and enchanted us—animals in particular have been closely connected with the gods and have performed a central role in shaping our spirituality. Even in the modern world, animals are intrinsically linked with abstract concepts. All manner of creatures may appear in our dreams, helping us to understand our own subconscious minds. Some act as omens of good fortune whilst others forebode ambiguous luck.

The call of the wild

The lion is one of the most powerful animals in both nature and symbolism. In dreams, a placid lion denotes personal gain, but if the lion is angered the omen is reversed and it means possible loss.

The tiger (*left*) is another fearsome animal of dreamlore. Those stalked by tigers in their dreams should guard themselves against dangers lurking just out of view. If you run from the beast it means that you have failed to confront your problems, but those who stand up to the beast should take encouragement, as it indicates that resolve and determination will eventually prevail when troubles seem to surround you.

Another favorite is the elephant, known for its longevity and powers of memory. If encountered in a dream, it is considered a talisman of business acumen and innovation.

Friends to man

Domestic animals hold different connotations to those of wild creatures. They are an important part in our lives, and thus command a special place in modern dreamlore. In dreams they represent elements of arguably the most primal of all energies—love. To see a horse running

above *Orchids are said to represent animal passion. Their vivid colors and phallic shapes symbolize wantonness and debauchery. This example of a wild bee orchid is well chosen, as the plant's velvety flowerheads serve to lure bees to its pollen receptors by the ruse of sexual deception.*

TRAPPED Caged animals represent the death of innocence—that reality will soon intrude upon an idealistic situation. To escape the cage means to move forward with your life and escape the shackles of your mind.

Animals and Plants

right Animals have long been regarded as possessing an insight into the natural world that mankind has lost. Thus dreams featuring animals often hark back to a primeval longing for a simpler existence —perhaps the kind that our ancestors, the primates, experienced.

below To dream of a dolphin symbolizes the emotional attachment of the psyche—their interest in us (swimming toward or away from us) serves to differentiate between the profound and the superficial.

free foretells a passionate affair, whilst to dream of riding bareback indicates a desire to be overwhelmed. However, to be thrown from a horse is not an auspicious omen and may well indicate that "love offered" could end up being "love scorned."

Dogs symbolize a desire to balance approval with integrity. If a dreamer envisions a dog licking a wound, it is thought to portend (however unhygenically) the curing of an ill—either physical or mental.

To dream of a cat can represent a warning of treachery and double dealings; however, the appearance of our feline friend can also be seen as signaling an independent spirit and a desire to break free from orthodox constraints.

Sea creatures

Images of deep water represent profound, often subconscious, thoughts; thus those creatures that live in this silent domain are intrinsically linked with such ideas. Crabs have thick shells

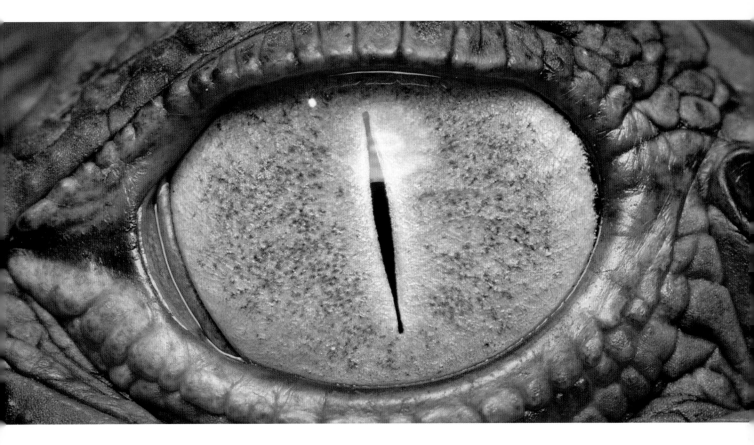

above To envisage a crocodile may represent possible danger lurking beneath the surface—perhaps friends, family, or colleagues that are not all they seem to be and are serving their own interests, not yours.

and fierce claws, and warn those that dream of them to beware of anyone who uses bravado and threats to get what they want.

To dream of catching fish denotes the pursuit of wealth; a fish that has been caught but escapes illustrates fortitude to overcome one's problems. To dream of a fish out of water denotes that the sleeper feels overwhelmed by problems, or has recently been placed in an uncomfortable situation.

Whales are no longer the feared "monsters of the deep" and are now viewed as symbols of peace and inner strength. They warn of inner struggles, but also of a better life to come after these troubles have been acknowledged and finally vanquished.

Enemies in the shadow

Creatures that terrify our conscious minds actually have colorful and positive subliminal meanings, and are not something that should be feared. The classic example of this is the snake—in dreams, they actually represent regeneration and renewal.

For many, spiders are the very stuff of nightmares but in dreams their influence should be seen as far from terrifying. Dream-spiders often appear when the sleeper needs to make an important decision and they can also denote the dreamer's tremendous tenacity in pursuing an objective. A spider's web can represent home life and the dreamer's ability to understand and heal family rifts.

Bizarrely, it was once believed that if you dreamt of swallowing a spider, you would actually awake the next morning with a magical way with words!

SERPENTS Some people still argue that snakes in dreams denote loss, sacrifice, ill fortune, and evil but nothing could be farther from the modern view—that snakes signify losing bad habits of old and starting over.

Animals and Plants

The dreamlore of birds

Different birds have different meanings within dreams. Surprisingly, one of the most auspicious of all birds is the ungainly pelican. In dreamlore the "pelican in its piety" is a symbol of self-sacrifice and may appear when the dreamer has important decisions to make—which involve them putting the needs of others before themselves.

Conversely, the cuckoo is the antithesis of the pelican. In nature the cuckoo fosters its eggs upon other unsuspecting birds, and thus to dream of a cuckoo implies deception either on the sleeper's part or someone else's.

Crows and ravens can signify betrayal or abandonment while a dove signifies that the sleeper's worries are unfounded.

Creatures of the dust

Dreaming of a swarm of small animals signifies that individual vexations, that alone could have been easily dealt with, have multiplied to such an extent that they now threaten to overwhelm you. However, if a swarm is seen dispersing, this is a sign that the sleeper can overcome their problems by dealing with them in a methodical manner, issue by issue.

To envisage a moth in flight warns against the rashness of letting your heart rule your head, while dreaming of many ants foretells the promise of a highly successful business or a mutual venture.

left Caterpillars can be joyous omens of an improved life, suggesting that just as the caterpillar emerges as a butterfly, we too can become better people.

Unloved and unwelcomed!

In life flies are seen as a petty annoyance, but in dreams they can forecast greater problems and can signify disturbance to the pattern of everyday life. If they are seen as a swarm, this suggests that the dreamer is being overwhelmed by problems.

Rats and mice offer less sinister omens and invariably signify news. Dreaming of a rodent standing on its hind legs looking at you heralds the arrival of important information, whilst to see one scurrying away indicates that the dreamer is having vital information kept from them by others.

Toads were associated with witchcraft and therefore still have an unenviable reputation. But in modern dreamlore, they can serve as an ally; if the creature should appear in your dream, it signifies that you should look for the true character in someone (good or bad) and not be fooled by first impressions.

Stingers and swarmers

Dreams in which you are stung symbolize the pain you have caused others, or will cause someone through your misdeeds. Wasps are the most likely agents of a sting, and to dream of them forewarns you that gossip may be being spread about you by people you trust. Dreams in which a hornet appears signal serious disruption in a friendship or some sort of complication in a financial transaction.

To see bees making honey implies a potential financial reward. However, if you dream of killing a bee, it may herald the loss of a close friendship, or a lover parted by jealousy.

Mosquitoes in dreams represent people who, in your waking life, are trying to get all they can from you without giving anything in return—literally, "blood suckers." If a scorpion is seen with its stinger raised ready to attack, the sleeper may be keeping a dark secret that is about to rebound and "sting" them.

above *Scorpions are extremely potent for their size and symbolize unforeseen problems that have been allowed to get out of all proportion!*

Be wary of scorpions —their appearance in dreams is never good news.

PLANTS AND FLOWERS

The frequency with which we dream about flowers and plants is testimony to the hold they exert within dreamlore, and strong feelings are engendered by them. If we are content, we may dream of sitting in a summer's garden surrounded by dazzling flowers, but if sad or confused we may dream we are lost in the darkness of a vast forest.

The close connection between plants and nature means they are often associated with strong natural desires. These may be positive (roses symbolize affection) or negative—dead flowers denote disappointment.

Dream flowers

Roses are regarded as flowers of love, and in dreamlore they retain this symbolic link. To dream of receiving the "Queen of Flowers" still remains a symbol of a strong physical or spiritual attachment to a current partner or friend.

In Christian iconography, the lily has close links with the Virgin Mary. Its white petals were commonly spread on the bed of newly-weds to symbolize the virginal purity of the bride. However, in dreamlore the lily carries a mixed message of sadness tinged with joy.

right *Plants are the very embodiment of Mother Nature. They feed us, heal us, and decorate our homes. Throughout history, people have used plants both for their own purposes and in the worship of their gods. Even today, they hold many connotations.*

right *To dream of walking in a field of wildflowers is suggestive of youth and vitality, but also cautions the dreamer to "seize the hour."*

BEAUTY BEGUILES...
Once the rose has become a scarlet hip, the vicious nature of its tangled web of thorns emerges plainly into view.

The color of flowers has its own dream iconography. To see white flowers in sleep indicates purity and the transcendent; yellow blooms are linked to wealth and majesty, but, by extension, envy; red is indicative of passion and sexual chemistry, whilst purple flowers denote chastity and feminine spirituality.

Wildflowers

In the realms of sleep, the poppy is often viewed with a certain hopeful trepidation and seen as a symbol of fleeting happiness; just as a poppy when picked will soon wilt and die, these flowers presage a brief romance, albeit one filled with tenderness and love.

The primrose symbolizes eternal love, comfort, and peace. Cowslips promise success in the workplace and strong bonds of friendship, whilst violets speak of joyous occasions and matrimonial devotion. The presence of buttercups, dandelions, and daisies in dreams signifies the many small blessings we can all too easily take for granted.

Humble forget-me-nots are dream heralds of everlasting love and hope. In dreamlore, they underlie the strong bonds of fidelity to a current partner, or deep feelings for someone from your past that you will never be able to forget or perhaps let go of fully.

above Poppies are closely linked with sleep. Morphine, extracted from poppy seeds, derives its name from Morpheus, who was thought to help promote sleep.

right *Hops are closely linked to sleep. Many natural sleep-inducing remedies include hops, and their presence in the recipe are said to inspire sweet dreams.*

far right *In dreams, cacti's thorns warn against small differences of opinion that might lead to a much larger rift.*

Crops and harvest

Considering their importance to our survival, it is little wonder that crops and their successful harvesting remain an important focus of our sleeping as well as waking lives.

Corn was believed to be the offspring of the sun and the earth, and was considered symbolic of both fertility and divine wisdom. In dream almanacs, it was closely linked with emotional fulfillment as well as financial reward. Wheat holds close connections with loving partnerships, and even more auspiciously, the fertility of an enlightened mind.

Vineyards and orchards represent long life and prosperity, though to see yourself picking the fruit is sometimes regarded as an unfavorable omen and warns of hardship through folly. To dream of sowing seeds implies a period of personal hardship that will ultimately result in prosperity.

Prickles, poisoners, and stings

Not all plants are content to be mere objects of decorative adoration; some have no intention

of simply "looking pretty," but instead have developed intricate ways to defend themselves. Such plants are viewed by many with distrust and even scorn, but their place in dreamlore ranks alongside their more attractive cousins. For example, unlike the edible mushroom, toadstools encountered in dreams act as a warning against unhealthy desires or the pursuit of vainglorious pleasure. If they are seen to be eaten, their meaning is even more

BEST PROTECTION *Rowan berries were said to protect you from witchcraft, and today their scarlet fruits are believed to guard against trickery and deception.*

To become tangled in a tree's roots is redolent of our basest earthly desires.

sinister, foretelling degradation and disgrace. Poisonous mistletoe heralds fecundity and sexual potency, and to dream of presenting a lover with a mistletoe bough suggests the strengthening of important bonds of romance and friendship.

Brambles, nettles, and teasels are often seen in dreams blocking our paths. These represent troubles and misfortune, though they should not be viewed with alarm—they are not signs of ills to come, but a suggestion to try to solve the problems in our waking lives.

Talismanic plants

Trees have always been blessed with talismanic qualities and to see a tree in your dreams is generally a happy omen that portends the fulfillment of one's hopes and aspirations.

The oak is known for its strength, and it is commonly believed that to dream of one whilst pregnant will herald the birth of a strong, healthy baby. However, it is also said to be talismanic in the devotion of love.

Yew is a tree whose presence in a dream emphasizes gravitas and a need for careful consideration if new ventures are to be undertaken or fresh plans made. Hawthorn is said to ease the passage of speech.

Seed heads, seeds, and fruits have their own meaning within sleep. For example, sloes from the blackthorn bush may look appetizing, but they have a sour taste to metaphorically warn the dreamer about taking things at face value.

right *The ash tree is considered to be sacred in Celtic mythology, and today it symbolizes the joy of the intellect such as the use of language and word-play.*

THE PHYSICAL SELF

Our sleeping thoughts revolve around us, and therefore we are always the most important subject of our own dream. So the symbolism of our physical body, the effects of life and death upon it, and the mental image we have of ourselves is ripe for interpretation. Most people think they know their bodies well, so it seems surprising then that we rarely appear in our dreams as we do in waking life. We often dream of ourselves slimmer, more muscular, or with larger breasts, but such a self-image is a reflection of how we *desire* to be seen, and every part of the body offers revelations.

Body lore

The appearance of the neck in dreams warns the sleeper to use their head (signifying "reason") as well as their heart in matters of love, and not to throw themselves blindly into a relationship without first considering the repercussions.

Shoulders represent a burden which we are happy to accept, and which will give us a new perspective on life. To envisage your back in a dream implies that others may be plotting against you. The chest is an area representative of strength and authority. To imagine you have a powerful torso is a sign of empowerment for men, whilst women who dream of their own breasts are considered to be confident and high achievers.

The visualization of legs and feet in a dream symbolizes the foundation and basis of the sense of stability in our lives.

above *In sleep your psyche can take you to any destination. To visualize a footprint (as here, on the lunar surface) confirms your arrival somewhere. Be sure to remember the location for, exciting or dull, it may reflect opportunities offered up to you in waking life.*

The face

Eyes have been described as the "windows to the soul," and this imagery is mirrored in dreamlore. Blue eyes suggest fickleness and warn of inconsistency in love. Hazel eyes tell the dreamer to beware those who would use flattery to deceive, and brown eyes caution against placing too much faith in what is "said" as opposed to what is actually "done."

ALL SEEING EYE To see this image (featured on the dollar bill) in a dream cautions the sleeper against dishonorable actions, telling them that they could well be putting their own self-interest above all else.

right *Our faces are the part of ourselves that most clearly display the emotions we feel. To see the face of a friend or relative, especially someone recently deceased, could signify the communication of a message. If they are smiling, this could mean they are happy with you or they have found contentment. If sad, they may be trying to express their displeasure at some unworthy action.*

Mouths reflect concerns the dreamer may have about others talking about them behind their back. An open mouth can signify the onset of an argument, a laughing mouth foretells reckless behavior, and a closed mouth with luscious lips indicates sexual desire.

What lies within

Dreaming of organs of the body relates to our physical wellbeing. To dream of the stomach is commonly a reflection of the worries in waking life. Dreaming of the liver may imply a need to detoxify our bodies or change our diets; lungs, said to be linked to the soul, reflect concerns we have about lost spirituality.

The heart in dreamlore represents sincerity and compassion. Due to its connection with romance, a dream may herald the start of a new romance or the rekindling of a previous one. To bleed in a dream symbolizes a loss of power.

above *Dreams of growing fat are sometimes taken to be a positive sign of increased prosperity, yet they could simply demonstrate worries for one's health and fitness.*

Life's little imperfections

Many of us fear losing our hair. In dreamlore thinning hair can represent financial loss for men, but conversely implies success in a woman's career.

To age in a dream means that you will make wise and informed decisions, while to become significantly younger suggests that you are currently acting with a reckless disregard for the facts.

Upon reflection

Naturally we tend to place ourselves at the center of our dreams but sometimes our physical features are altered for the better or for the worse. On occasion, we may see images of ourselves through the eyes of others. For example, fear of embarrassment often dictates the way we behave during our waking lives, and dreams where we embarrass ourselves can be highly unsettling.

Two of the most common dreams of imagined humiliation are undressing in public or finding oneself naked in a public place. While these dreams may seem cruel on the surface, they are often just the mind's way of unburdening repressed anxieties, often forged during childhood, which have been allowed to fester and multiply over time.

Called into being

Many women dream of being pregnant. Such dreams may be simple wish fulfillment, a desire to have children, or to start a family. For others, however, the dream prophesies new beginnings—perhaps a start of a new project that has been constantly put off.

Dreams of giving birth imply that the dreamer will discover a new talent previously unknown to them. If the labor is perceived to be difficult, the sleeper may expect to encounter problems along this path of self-discovery.

MAYBE BABY? Men can dream about being pregnant—some believe this is the male wishing to reconnect to their "child within," but others simply believe that it is his paternal instincts awakening.

below *Mirrors in dreams reflect not how we look, but beguile or flatter the sleeper as their vanity dictates. As a general rule, interpret a mirror dream by reversing its apparent meaning.*

LIFE AND DEATH

Our health, and that of our friends and family, is one of our greatest concerns and this worry permeates our dreams. In fact, such images usually serve to help us, highlighting problems we might ignore in our waking lives.

While dreams of illness very rarely portend poor health, if you have recurring dreams about a specific area of your body, it may be advisable to consult a doctor. Although rare, during restful sleep, your brain can occasionally highlight problems that your waking mind may have missed or overlooked.

Doctors and nurses

Due to the role they play in helping cure us in our waking lives, doctors are viewed as positive omens in dreams. To see oneself visiting a doctor is a sign that any minor problems the dreamer is experiencing in life will soon be settled. To meet a doctor in a social capacity is auspicious, suggesting good health and prosperity. If a doctor comes to your home, it indicates that friends and family will rally round you to help sort out any problems you are currently experiencing. If the sleeper imagines

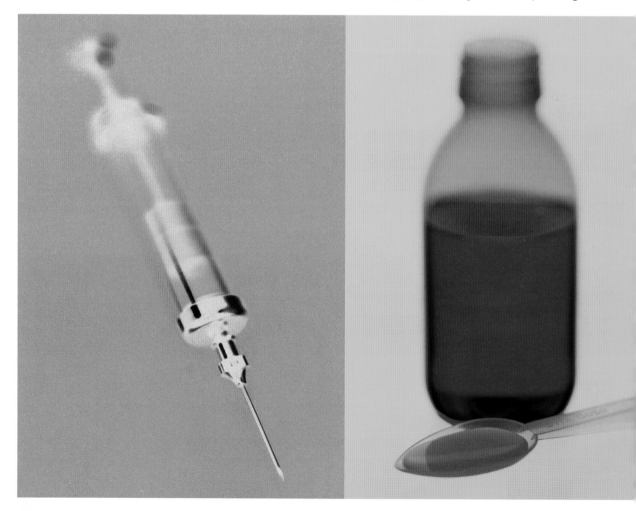

No one likes medical procedures but they are good for us—the same applies to such imagery appearing in our dreams.

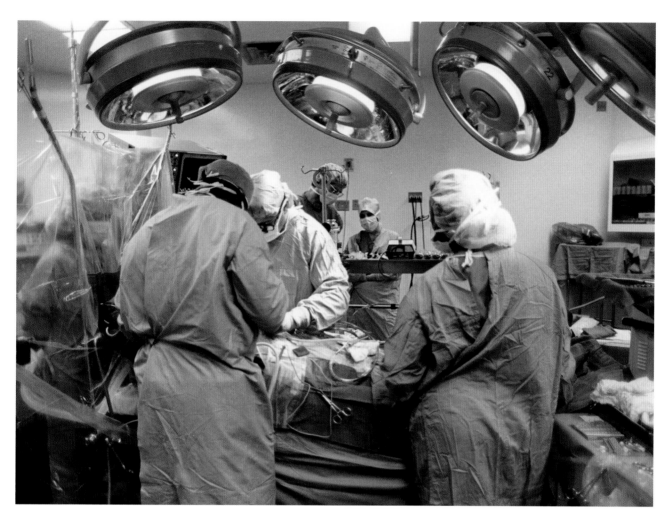

that they are gravely ill, it is usually taken as a sign that they remain healthy in waking life—an example of the subconscious mind's "contrary thought," where anxieties are dealt with by the expediency of imagining a worst-case scenario.

Like doctors, nurses can be viewed as encouraging figures within dreamlore. If they are viewed holding a baby or a small child, it should be taken as a sign that the dreamer will enjoy a new and rewarding friendship. If a nurse is seen entering or leaving the house, it is usually a portent of balanced health.

"It's for your own good!"

Simply dreaming of hospitals can make the sleeper feel uncomfortable and anxious.

Their appearance in our dreams may seem unlucky because they might imply that a friend or family member will face a traumatic time; however, rather than being harbingers of gloom, such dreams serve to remind us of our obligations toward others.

Medical instruments have their own symbolism. Scalpels warn the sleeper not to take risks with their health, stethoscopes forebode indiscretion, and thermometers remind us of the responsibility we have to others.

Dreams of illness and infirmity

Dreams of illness and infirmity can be greatly unsettling but such dreams are merely seeking to highlight our inner fears and concerns, or

above *Dreams of operations are a sign that the sleeper needs to take stock of their life and reassess their priorities.*

The Physical Self

The Physical Self

right *Dreams of dying can be unsettling, but they serve to warn us that we are under threat from an external force. This may be a rival who undermines us at work, a rival in love, or even someone who drains us of our emotional life-force.*

warn us of dangers which if acted upon can be avoided. In dreams where the sleeper appears to be hurt, it is important to take note of the intensity of the pain.

If light, it may suggest that the sleeper will have to suffer a small degree of discomfort—occasionally physical, but more often emotional or spiritual—to achieve a planned goal. However, if the pain is intense, the dreamer should reassess whether their plans are worth the heavy price they will have to pay in order to achieve them.

Dreams in which your body feels tired or strained are a sign that you are taking life too seriously. Fevers and fits symbolize that you are worrying unnecessarily over trivial matters and need to reassess your priorities.

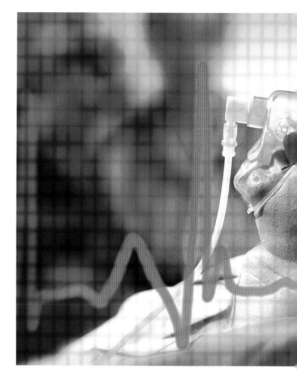

Near death experiences

The question of the existence of near death experiences is controversial. While there are detractors who argue that such visions are more inner-body hallucinations than outer-body experiences, there are many men and women who have "died" that are convinced otherwise.

An outer-body experience supposedly occurs when the soul leaves the body. This may be for several minutes or simply a fraction of a second. Such dreamlike experiences occur

when the heart stops beating for a short time during trauma or major surgery.

While this might seem frightening to some, most who have undergone a near death experience are left with a feeling of great inner peace—all of us fear death and the prospect of an afterlife is comforting for many of us. In dreamlore, similar visions of a "life after death" are symbolic of new beginnings.

Near death A common theme of a near death experience is the feeling of leaving your body and traveling toward another place—often a radiant light at the end of a tunnel. The second is a return to the body as you are revived, often with an intense feeling of disappointment.

The final curtain

Dreaming of death is not a bad omen. To see yourself attending a family funeral is, paradoxically, a sign that they are in good health and may soon be celebrating a happy event. Meanwhile, to dream of your own funeral symbolizes that a particularly difficult phase will soon be over—you have buried the old so it's time to welcome in the new!

Dreams of neglected graves imply that the sleeper has secrets they wish to conceal, while cracked or fallen tombstones warn that ambitions should never be held above personal contentment. Dreaming of your own grave can be traumatic and symbolizes problems in your waking life that you are literally trying to bury.

A neglected grave implies the sleeper has secrets they wish to conceal.

THE EMOTIONAL SELF

Our feelings are at the heart of everything. Whether it be emotions about family and friends or which public figures we dream of as detailed later in this chapter, our sleeping thoughts can reveal much about who we are —none more so though than our sexual feelings. Erotic dreams do not always simply represent our fantasies, but can expose unknown sides of our character. For example, those that regularly fantasize about pleasing themselves can be more interested in self-gratification than the needs of others. But this is merely a glimpse of our erotic dreamscapes…

Seductive desires

In dreams, as in life, flirting can be a sign of your intentions or simply a harmless diversion. To dream of flirting with a friend or a colleague at work should not be taken to imply a desired outcome, but is more usually taken to suggest a desire for more excitement or challenges in your working life.

To see yourself kissing someone that you really like is usually wish fulfillment and should not be taken as a sign that they return your feelings; more fortuitous might be a dream kiss with a mysterious partner—this may well symbolize the start of an exciting and new relationship.

Dreaming of undressing in front of a lover shows that you are comfortable in their presence and are ready to share your secrets with that person or to commit to them at a deeper emotional level.

Dreams of having sex in unusual positions or places suggest that the sleeper longs for more excitement and passion, and should seek new ways to enliven romance in the waking world. Having an affair within the realms of sleep also suggests a desire for greater sexual liberation—although not necessarily with a fresh romance.

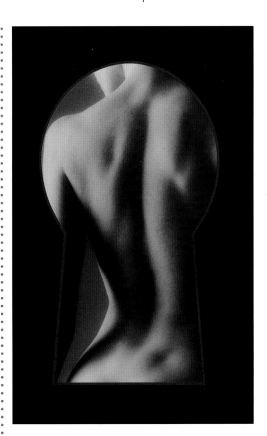

above *Dreaming of a lock and key where the key is placed in the lock corresponds intimately to the roles of male and female.*

opposite page *Our emotional selves are complex and worthy of exploration. While the "court jester" illustrated here represents seering honesty (see page 64), there are so many more different sides to us and our emotions.*

above right *Freud believed that all dreams represented our deepest desires, which in adults were invariably wish fulfillment dreams focused on sexual activity.*

below right *The guilt of supposed sexual impotency in men is a dream that invariably reveals an inability to cope with the events of the dreamer's life. Don't despair—if the dreamer tackles such issues methodically, they will be surprised at how easily they can regain control of their lives.*

Common sexual themes

Role play is a common theme in dreams of an erotic nature. Nurses or doctors represent the compulsion of another domain over your body; policemen and women exert authority and discipline, whilst strippers or the burlesque are perceived to cover more traditional territory.

Dream fantasies involving prostitutes or orgies represent a desire for sexual experimentation, but their omens are seldom encouraging—the deep well of past morality surrounding such behavior.

Dreaming of sex with a member of the same gender does not necessarily reveal homosexual tendencies. Often the people we choose to sleep with merely personify characteristics we find attractive or long for ourselves.

Dream fantasies of bondage represent a desire to relinquish control. It is an especially common dream for people who have high-powered jobs and who secretly long to hand over control to someone else for a while.

Measuring up to sexual anxiety

The most common form of sexual anxiety is a fear of inadequacy. Dreams of sexual inadequacy directly mirror the fears the sleeper has in their waking lives. Sometimes the dream may exaggerate the problem out of all proportion, making it seem far worse than it really is. This may be compounded by the dreamer imagining themselves exposed in public, or being laughed at by a partner; however, this apparent sign of sexual inadequacy is rarely sexually motivated and is far more likely to point to other areas in the sleeper's life that they consider to be a failure—perhaps mounting financial debt or a reversal of career opportunity.

Voyeurs spy on other people's experiences for their own sexual gratification and dreams featuring yourself as the voyeur display unease with your sexual performance and a need for sympathetic reassurance from your partner.

True love

Dreaming of love may reveal secret passions or a longing for a fresh dimension to our lives. Even those already in a happy and caring relationship may dream of falling in love with someone new. This is seldom a sign that we are unhappy with our current partner, but that we are looking for an added element to our life —this might simply be the desire to learn a new language, or it could be a signal to travel to strange and exotic locations.

To dream of falling in love with someone that is unattainable is a sign of future disappointment. Although they may appear tantalizingly close, their love will always be beyond your reach.

Dreams of first love are particularly poignant because they can hold so many bitter-sweet memories. In dreamlore, first love represents innocence and, as such, demonstrates a longing to return to a simpler time.

Love soured

Dreaming of the breakdown of a relationship is not an omen that your partnership is doomed, but may simply reflect problems that exist in our waking lives that have filtered haphazardly into our dreamscape.

Dreaming that you and your partner are becoming increasingly alienated from each other is a sign that your relationship is under strain. Given such prompts, it is advisable to talk to your partner about what you both want out of life, and how to build on your relationship and make it stronger.

Dreams of being jilted by one we love are often merely a sign of our own anxieties. However, in some cases the omens may be fortuitous, predicting a chance to start anew with someone who will prove a far better match. Divorce may be harrowing in real life, but in dreamlore it signals independent actions and success through one's own efforts.

above *To dream of meeting someone and developing a mutual attraction suggests the dreamer is confident.*

right *Dreaming that someone is spreading rumors about us, or those we love, may indicate that we secretly know something is wrong in our waking relationships.*

The Emotional Self

THOSE CLOSE TO US

The importance of friends and family to us means that their appearance in our dreams holds the power to be either comforting or distressing. While they may appear to symbolize security and support, dreams can warp events and personalities to leave us feeling confused. To see those we love endangered can be particularly uncomfortable—though this should never be seen as a portent of suffering,

but merely our subconscious' way of reminding us how much they mean to us and never to take them for granted.

The dreamer's family

To dream of your parents demonstrates a longing for security or approval. Returning to the warm embrace of a loving mother or father suggests that we are finding it hard to cope with certain elements of our waking lives and seek the comfort that only our parents can provide. Mothers personify love and support, while fathers reflect a desire for authority or protection.

Sons and daughters reflect the pride we feel—not merely in our families, but also in our wider achievements. If the dreamer

views themselves as a father with their son, it is important to note the child's actions and feelings—the sleeper's aspirations may often be reflected in said child's actions. A mother dreaming of her daughter again holds up a mirror to the dreamer but the focus in the pairing is on the sleeper's fears and hopes for the future.

Brothers and sisters are often the ones we turn to in troubled times, and to view one's sibling in a dream is an encouraging sign of fortitude and the ability to overcome problems in the face of adversity.

Grandparents are synonymous with wisdom and knowledge. It is advisable to listen to any message they impart, especially for those who have unresolved issues in their waking lives.

Bonds of friendship

Our friends are the family we choose, those with whom we can share our emotions and aspirations, joys, and fears. In dreamlore,

below *If a father dreams of their son, it is important to observe the child's behavior and emotions—they can reflect the dreamer's own strengths and weaknesses.*

however, the role of these people—who often become closer to us than our own families—is varied and complex. Dreaming of meeting an old friend may simply be a nostalgic longing for a lost friendship, but it can also hint at a sense of loss in our current lives, or suggest a desire for moral support and guidance through a particularly difficult time.

Often in our dreams we are helped or supported by a "friend" who we do not know in waking life. This may reflect a feeling that our current friends are not truly listening to us, although it is more likely the psyche's reminder to the sleeper that we owe a duty of care to those around us—not only to those that we love and care for, but anyone in need of our help.

To dream of being betrayed by a friend appears sinister, but it is not a sign of ill in real life—usually it is an illustration of the insecurity of losing those who we love.

LOVE'S LABOR Anxiety and fear for those we love can often creep into our dreams and lead us to believe that they are in mortal danger. These dreams though are simply expressions of usually healthy concern, and should not be regarded as being predictive. If you feel shaken by such dreams though, talk to the person you witnessed in the dream to allay your fears.

VISIONARY FIGURES

Dreaming of someone famous does not mean that we necessarily long for fame, but it is often a recognition that we wish to replicate their skill or an associated trait. This can prove a positive influence and can inspire us to strive for our own success.

In our dreams, we may also adopt many different personae. They reveal the

right *"The Magic Apple Tree" by Samuel Palmer, circa 1830. In this exquisite English masterpiece, the artist captures the dreamlike state of reality transformed into visionary abundance. The picture seems to mirror Palmer's own words, "we are like the chrysalis asleep, and dreaming of its wings."*

characteristics we may long to espouse—such as valor or reticence—yet they tell us more about the person we currently are, the wise man or the fool!

Images of self

We meet many people in our personal dreamscape, although they are often personifications of our own individual traits, emotions, or aspirations.

The hero is a particularly popular image and one the dreamer may feel a strong affinity toward. The hero may take the form of a movie star, action man, or fictional warrior, each possessing a certain facet that the dreamer longs to emulate. Although they are often

figures of wish fulfillment, sometimes heroes also reflect characteristics that the sleeper possesses of which they are currently unaware.

Images of a mask, or wearing a mask yourself, indicate that the dreamer is currently concealing, or wishes to hide, elements of themselves. To be seen to remove the mask suggests that they are gaining in the confidence they need to truly be themselves.

The image of a hermit, unsurprisingly, symbolizes solitude, and suggests that the sleeper longs to have more time to themselves. To be approached by a hermit suggests that the answer to one's problems lies internally rather than externally, and one should seek wisdom deep within oneself.

Finally, one of the most intriguing of all images of "self" is that of the fool. This talismanic image harks back many centuries to when fools alone were allowed *carte blanche* to criticize a king surrounded by impotent sycophants—thus the only unbiased and trustworthy advice came from the court jester. To encounter the fool is a sign that the dreamer has successfully balanced the two important elements of work and play.

Inspirational and authoritarian figures

While dreams of meeting famous people can be seen as simple wish fulfillment, the appearance of the people we admire in our dreams also tells us something about ourselves.

Often it is not the people that we meet in our dreams that are important, but the characteristics we associate with them. For example, dreaming of meeting a current President or Prime Minister may represent a desire for success. Likewise, movie stars and musicians imply a wish to emulate their skill and success. Such dream meetings may inspire you to take up an instrument yourself, to paint, dance, or sing—whatever it takes to start you on the career path or pursuit to eventually achieving your dreams. A word of warning though —to imagine that you regularly meet celebrities can have negative overtones. This is especially true if the sleeper sees themselves working for the celebrity. Such dreams hint at a feeling of inferiority and suggest that you feel overlooked or neglected in your waking life.

Figures of authority help shape our waking lives and their role in dreamlore is usually that

above *To dream of Mother Teresa may express a long-held desire to help others less fortunate than yourself.*

of guidance and support. Outside the family, teachers have arguably the greatest influence on our childhood lives and consequently they are etched on to our subconscious. The appearance of an old teacher in a dream is a sign that the dreamer requires structure in their life. They also warn us to seek the opinions of others we trust before making important decisions.

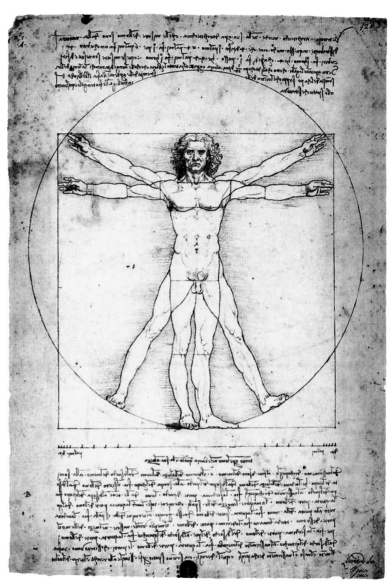

Policemen symbolize protection and security, and the appearance of a uniformed officer in our dreams is an omen that help may arrive from an unexpected source. They also warn those with an important decision to make to choose the option they know to be right, rather than the one that feels easiest.

Dreaming of a judge was once supposed to foretell the death of an enemy. However, their presence in a dream is now thought to signify the onset of a serious argument over a trivial matter.

above *Leonardo da Vinci drew this famous illustration of the Vitruvian man— dreaming of such a great artist could inspire you to start drawing your own creations.*

THE SPIRITUAL SELF

If the world were merely about pure physicality, it would be a dull place indeed, and one with seemingly no answers. We humans have always struggled to find such answers to the big questions regarding who and what we are. This has led to us exploring our spiritual side, examining our faith, fantasies, luck, and darker issues such as violence. The dreamscape offers a chance to navigate such thoughts and feelings and plays a vital role in helping us understand our spiritual sides—especially when it comes to the religions of the world.

Faith and worship

Sections of the Qur'an were revealed to Mohammed in a dream; Jacob (the father of the twelve tribes of Israel) dreamt that he climbed a ladder to heaven and heard God promise him the land of Israel; while the Hindu text *Brahmavaiarta Purana* is a guide to interpreting the will of the gods through dreams. On every continent, there are people who believe that their god can communicate through images received in sleep.

Today, dreams are generally considered to be more closely linked to our psyche than to divine command, yet dreams of a religious nature still hold potency for believers. If we dream that God has spoken to us—while this is unlikely to be a divine message—it may be something that our subconscious wants us to examine, and should be explored.

Symbols of faith

Churches, temple, synagogues, and mosques are buildings of great spiritual importance; they hold an impressive sense of magnitude and reverence, even for non-believers. In dreams they are usually interpreted to represent our soul. Seeing an empty place of worship in a dream, devoid of furniture or decoration, is

above *An angel appearing in a dream can offer you comfort if you are struggling with sorrow—or perhaps it is there to impart a message.*

right To dream of a saint—such as the famous St George—signifies spiritual protection and help in a noble venture.

below The altar is the focal point of the church, and to imagine one in a dream implies the discovery of inner peace. To stand with your back to an altar, however, forebodes approaching sorrows.

a sign that the sleeper has abandoned the beliefs they once held dear; whilst to envision a church or mosque elaborately decorated and thronged with a large number of worshippers can suggest a reawakening of the dreamer's own spirituality.

Images inside many religious buildings are also significant. The font in a church is a symbol of acceptance into the Christian faith, and represents ideas of renewal or redirection in dreamlore.

In Christianity, bells are used to call people to church and in the realms of sleep they symbolize the arrival of good news. In Islam, minarets are a sign of obedience and devotion and in dreams are known to represent news of a spiritual nature.

Flowers may be viewed decorating a church or temple, and their appearance in a religious context denotes a reawakening of the dreamer's inner spirituality. A candle

burning steadily represents consistency of belief, while statues embody intuitive awareness, telling the sleeper to listen to their instincts no matter what troubling doubts they might experience along the way.

Dreaming of a cross tells the sleeper (whether they are a believer or not) that, although fate may have conspired against them, their period of ill luck will soon end. To dream of a holy book such as the Bible or the Qur'an indicates discretion and sensitivity—whilst to swear upon one tells the dreamer that despite criticism, their current actions are correct.

Heaven and hell

Dreaming of heaven is a sign of elevation; this may be a development of one's spiritual beliefs, or in a temporal sense can signify a promotion at work or a genuine improvement in one's social situation.

Images of hell are far less comforting. Dreaming of such a torturous place directly reflects the state of the sleeper's mind, highlighting troubles that may be tormenting them. These dreams often rely upon the savagery of medieval imagery to "haunt" people who know they have transgressed. Recurring dreams of hell indicate that the dreamer needs to rectify these "sins" during their waking lives in order to salve their conscience.

"He who would valiant be"

Images of pilgrims and martyrs represent those who have put their faith before worldly desires. Their role in dreamlore is to try and steer us toward the course of a "better life."

For many, to envision undertaking a pilgrimage in a dream is a sign that the sleeper believes they have transgressed and need to atone for their "sin." For others it may be a sign that they wish to take time away from the hubbub of everyday life to discover their true selves or to pursue a personal goal. If you are seen to go on a pilgrimage in a dream, try to remember those that assisted you and the people who hindered your progression—they will have distinct character traits to be found in those we encounter in waking life.

Priests, rabbis, and imams are all representative of people who have dedicated their lives to the service of their god. In dreams they may act as confidants, teachers, or even parental figures—in each case the role that they assume is important. To imagine being taught by one suggests the dreamer is seeking guidance, whilst to be comforted by one is a sign they are reaching out for support in a venture they feel unworthy to complete alone.

Martyrs have made the ultimate sacrifice, and if they appear in a dream it may be considered an omen that the sleeper will need to sacrifice certain elements of their temporal self to satisfy their spiritual integrity.

above *The word "hell" is derived from "hel," the Teutonic word for "to conceal." This verb is very apt for those who are plagued with images of the fiery place (as illustrated here)—dreaming of hell can mean that you need to uncover something that is causing you great upset.*

If you dream of talking to a pilgrim, it suggests that you have problems that can only be solved by outside intervention.

above *The appearance of a unicorn in your dream may indicate a close friendship with a member of the opposite sex, which will seem like the union of two souls.*

right *To dream of a demon implies that the sleeper has a guilty secret that still haunts their subconscious.*

FABLES AND FANTASIES

Myths and magic have become increasingly less important in today's society. Whilst our ancestors would have believed in the existence of mythical creatures, such beasts are now relegated to the pages of children's stories. Despite this, their echoes still frequent our dreams, and often visions that we would regard as too fantastical for waking life find a place in the dreamscape.

Heavenly messengers

Our dreams are a veritable treasure trove of religious symbolism. The most significant is the arrival of an angel in your dream, which may not simply be to impart a message to you (*see opposite picture's caption*)—their presence may also symbolize wisdom and protection. When the dreamer feels upset or alone in the world, angels can act as guardians to the vulnerable—looking over them and empowering them with the energy and the will required to improve their situation.

Monstrous visitations

Our psyche comprises many conflicting components and the darker elements that we consciously suppress in waking life are left to fester. In our dreams, we may loosen the leash on these sinister factors and they can become manifest in our dreams.

Today, dreams of demons may have lost their connotations of eternal damnation, but they retain elements of a sense of moral corruption. Any encounter with diabolical sources in a dream can be interpreted to foreshadow a brush with temptation.

To dream of a vampire or werewolf warns the sleeper that someone, or something, is depleting the dreamer's spiritual force— perhaps a burden of worry that is "draining them dry" of their psychic energy.

Baleful enchanters

In today's world there seems little room left for magic and mystery. Fairies, wizards, and

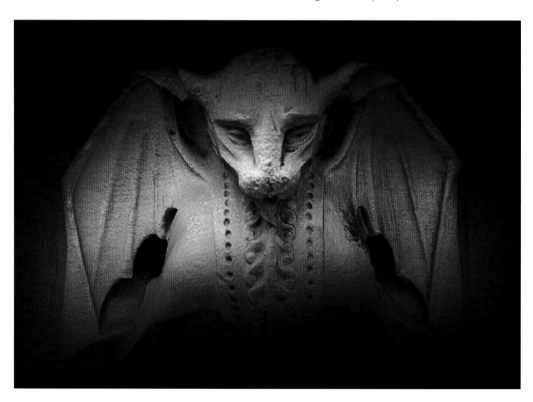

left *If an angel appears in your dream, it is advisable to take note of the message they impart. Angels may serve to steer you in the correct direction, warn you of potential danger, or reprimand you for past wrongs. Whatever the case, the dreamer should take their advice seriously.*

ogres no longer fill us with the literal sense of "enchantment" that they once did. In our dreams, however, these mystic creatures still retain some degree of influence and should never be dismissed as merely the imagery of a childish imagination.

Originally fairies were malevolent creatures that played tricks on mankind in order to hurt us. In dreamlore they retain much of this traditional imagery, warning us to beware those who appear to be assisting us, but who are in reality acting only for their own gain.

Similarly, will-o'-the-wisps and other fire spirits that used to lure travelers away from the safe paths through dangerous marshlands, also serve to warn us against those people that appear to be helping us, but who ultimately

want to see us fail. To encounter an ogre or giant in a dream is a sign that we will face problems in our waking lives. The larger or more fearsome the ogre, the harder the obstacle will be to overcome. The much misunderstood witch actually represents the sleeper's desire to embrace gnostic knowledge and a higher plane of consciousness.

Supernatural beasts

Dragons are one of the most potent animals in dreamlore and due to their power, they are emblematic of inner strength.

The griffin symbolizes vigilance whilst the sphinx acts as a warning against self deception. Centaurs caution against hasty behavior and making snap judgments.

GOTHICA Evil drives out evil so the presence of hideous gargoyles in our dreams should be viewed as a form of protection. They also indicate that we must guard against taking people at face value.

LUCK, SIGNS, AND SYMBOLS

below A horseshoe is a traditional symbol of good luck and in a dreamscape foretells success in the face of pessimism.

Mankind has an innate desire to seek out signs of good fortune wherever he looks. Throughout history he has applied mystical qualities to innate symbols—often based upon only the most spurious of links.

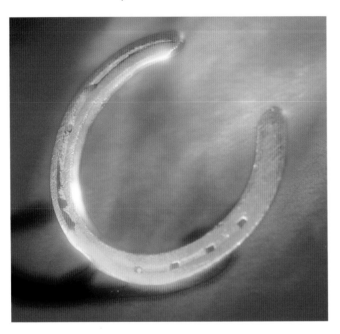

Talismanic objects

Simple objects have assumed talismanic powers because of our need to be reassured that the power of "luck" can be tamed and utilized to our own advantage. The horseshoe, four-leaf clover, and rabbit's foot all now symbolize good fortune, and because of the role they play in our subconscious, such objects have been absorbed into the symbolism of dreamlore.

The appearance of an hourglass in our dreams reminds us not to put off until tomorrow that which can be done today. Ladders are suggestive of an internal desire to strive for greater things. They demonstrate a desire for personal achievement, albeit in a professional or personal capacity. A fall from a ladder does not necessarily mean that you will be unsuccessful in your goals, but that you may need a greater degree of self-belief, or a change of tactics to achieve your desires.

The power of numbers

Numbers are a surprisingly common element in dreams. The number one is associated with the soul and denotes independence and individuality. The number two represents union and companionship and can signal the start of a new relationship or the cementing of an old.

Three represents creation, whilst four is the number of balance and stability. The number five signifies energy and is associated with a desire for adventure or freedom. Six is the number of harmony and equilibrium, stemming from the belief that the world was created in six days.

Seven is regarded as the luckiest number because it represents man's relationship with God, who instigated the seven virtues and seven sins. Eight in dreams is seen as a beginning of new horizons rather than decay.

below A crossed middle and second finger in a dream can be regarded as a sign of desire—the fingers mimicking the position of two lovers, one on top of the other other.

Finally, nine symbolizes growth and pregnancy (after the nine months a baby spends in its mother's womb) and often foretells a fresh development or a change of circumstance.

Color in your dreams

Colors have the ability to arouse powerful emotions and in dreams are highly symbolic. The color red represents excitement, anger, aggression, and sexual energy. It stirs up desires in the dreamer to act now and to put their emotions first so their desires can be fulfilled.

Blue is the color of spiritual understanding. It radiates compassion and strength of mind. It is the antithesis of red and warns the dreamer to act upon clear thoughts rather than simple reckless emotions.

Green represents healing and growth and, if seen when ill, is an extremely positive omen of improved health. However, for those in love,

it indicates jealousy and mistrust in either the dreamer or their partner.

Our inner psyche closely associates black with death, but in dreams it more commonly represents entrapment or the fear of the unknown. White opposes all aspects of black. It is the color of innocence, purity, and assurance. It suggests that the dreamer is currently making the right decisions in their life and that they should proceed as they believe appropriate, despite potential opposition.

above Many believe that numbers in dreams are a premonition of what horse to bet on or what numbers to play on the lottery. Even a dream in which the sleeper gambles and wins is not a sign of wealth, but rather an innate desire to achieve this. Numbers in dreams represent emotions and energies, not signs of how to achieve personal wealth.

Emerging from black into white in a dream is an encouraging omen and shows that the dreamer has the ability to break away from their fears.

VIOLENCE AND CONFLICT

Violence in our dreams is a way for the subconscious to unburden the anger and frustration we build up in waking life. Rather than being seen as an expression of sadistic intent, it is a means of unburdening emotions.

Inner wars

Dreaming of winning a battle means that your mind has reached a decision about a problem that has been troubling you—when you awake from such a dream, you should feel ready to tackle the predicament. To imagine losing a battle is a warning that you need to be cautious about how to properly solve your problems before implementing a "solution" that may rebound on you. Seeing yourself fighting in a war may be an outlet for the aggressive feelings you have suppressed in waking life, or an expression of an internal desire to prove yourself.

Our own dark angels

In dreams, emotions such as anger, envy, lust, and rage—"our own dark angels"—have more freedom to express themselves. To imagine that you kill someone is the most extreme form of violent outpouring. For many this is simply a case of releasing the latent anger that they may hold toward that person, but for others it is a demonstration of the sleeper's jealousy toward the "victim." By killing them they are symbolically trying to absorb those qualities that they secretly admire.

Brutal imagery in dreams rarely portends well if the sleeper takes pleasure from the violence.

SHIELD Dreams involving shields offer security—a dreamer may be facing problems in their waking life, but visualizing a shield promises them the strength of character to cope with whatever troubles come their way.

way of reproaching the dreamer for some guilty indiscretion or misdemeanor.

To envision a gallows or any other form of capital punishment is a warning against pursuing a course of action you know to be wrong—the gallows acts as an ominous signal that if you persist, the consequences will prove dire.

above *If the sleeper sees themselves placing a loved one in chains, it shows they are stifling them, or the sleeper's mistrust is destroying their relationship.*

right *To dream of shooting oneself in the foot is a warning not to bring trouble upon yourself through foolhardy actions—or you will end up paying!*

Choose your weapon

Weapons represent unaddressed frustration and aggression. If the dreamer sees themself striking another with a sword, they may be responding to a perceived attack on themself. Such aggressive self-defence is often inspired by feelings that the world is against them.

To find yourself attacked by someone wielding a dagger suggests that you feel scared or alone in your daily life; while to wrestle a dagger from an assailant is a sign that you will overcome your misfortunes.

Unjust ends

Dreams of being judged or standing trial can make the sleeper feel uncomfortable, denoting a natural dislike of being reproached or criticized. While the dreamer rarely knows what they are standing trial for, they are inevitably found guilty and punished. This is the psyche's

POSITIVE DREAMING

Many people believe that they have no control over their dreams, but this certainly need not be the case. As already observed, our dreams can tell us a great deal about our emotions, thoughts, and feelings. Keeping a dream diary is a good way of recording important symbolism, and by observing patterns and recurring themes, the sleeper can ensure that they recognize possible problems that may need attention—helping them eventually to improve both their waking and sleeping lives.

Remembering your dreams

It is important to record as much information as you can remember. Illustrated below is a list of subjects you may wish to include in your dream diary.

This list can be adapted to suit individual needs. For example, some people find it beneficial to grade their dream on a scale of 1 to 10—where 1 represents a terrifying nightmare, and 10 signifies a wonderfully uplifting dream. Others may like to add a box explaining how they felt before their dream and how they feel afterward. However it is adapted, a dream diary can grant the dreamer a significant insight into their emotional wellbeing and help them understand the nature of their dreams.

opposite page Try to release tensions and relax before falling asleep; it may help to visualize a special place that holds fond memories and has a calming effect upon your mind.

above and left *By noting as much information about your dream as possible, you should be able to understand your dreams better. However, even if you can't fill in all the suggested responses, it can still prove a useful exercise and "aide-memoire" to refer back to at a later date.*

DREAM DIARY

Date of dream:

Day of the week::

People involved in the dream:

Mood and feelings expressed:

Prominent colors:

What story did the dream enact?:

Problems and conflicts encountered:

How were problems dealt with?:

Did the dream occur in the past or present?:

Prominent symbols:

Repeated elements from past dreams:

How did the dream end?:

Conclusions:

above *Images of hell inhabited by grotesque monsters are common in nightmares because they represent the fear of retribution. However, as with all bad dreams, it is important to remember that, as frightening as such creatures can seem, they are designed for our personal benefit and can do us no physical harm.*

Banishing nightmares

Nightmares are the most misunderstood of all dreams. They are too often dismissed as representing nothing more than the distressed images of an over-imaginative mind.

Nightmares though are actually a healthy expression of deep-seated fears and tensions. Such images represent the dreamer's desire to deal with their problems rather than simply hiding from them. Often a nightmare will jolt you awake, sweating and in a disheveled state: regain your composure, then try to re-enter the dream, but this time forearmed with the confident knowledge that whatever your personal demons try to do to you, they will always lack the ability to harm you. Once they are seen for the impostors they truly are, you can begin to fight back. By far the most effective way of doing this is to use humor against your tormentors. For example, if your sleep is plagued by the vision of a vampire, take away his cloak and imagine a pink polka dot skirt in its place... really, what possible harm can he do to you now?

Another effective method for removing menace from nightmares (which works particularly well for children), is to draw the fears that haunt you in sleep on a sheet of paper, then add a bright sun in the sky, and turn the dour black of your worst fears into a multitude of vibrant colors; by adding jollity and humor to your imaginative armory, you create a strong weapon which becomes available for you to use whenever nightmares threaten.

Sweet dreams

Sweet dreams require a relaxing sleep. Here are some tips for achieving a good night's sleep.

1 Try not to worry about the amount of sleep you are managing to have. The quantity of sleep we need each night varies considerably. Often we overestimate the time we need to have actually slept.

2 Live an active life. If you have trouble falling asleep, it may be that your body is not tired. Exercise encourages the body to seek rest and will result in a deeper sleep.

3 Make sure you are fully relaxed. Before going to bed lessen your tension with a massage, do some light exercise, or go for a gentle walk.

4 Don't go to bed on a full stomach—leave two hours between your last meal and when you go to bed. Digestion can affect your sleeping pattern and may result in strange dreams.

5 Avoid stimulating your body. Caffeine drinks will prolong the time it takes for you to fall asleep, whilst alcohol and tobacco will prolong the period of light sleep when you are most likely to be disturbed by external influences.

6 Make sure your bed is comfortable—ideally the mattress should be firm but not hard.

7 Your bedroom should be neither too hot, nor too cold (a temperature between 60–65 °F/ 16–18 °C is generally considered comfortable). The room should be dark and all external noise should be as muffled as possible.

8 Keep a notebook by your bed to record any thoughts that are worrying you. There is little we can do about them late at night, but using a note pad allows us to "exorcise" our concerns.

9 Go to bed 30 minutes before going to sleep and read an untaxing book. It is important to relax your mind before going to sleep.

10 Relax. If you feel as though you can't sleep or you wake in the middle of the night, try not to worry about it. If you find that you still can't relax your mind, read some more, or try to think of a place or person that makes you feel safe and secure.

below Following the information listed on this page will help you explore and enjoy dreams that can be natural, sweet, and enjoyable. Just remember—there is nothing you can do about your concerns late at night so put them to one side and let go.

INDEX

EMOTION RAM'

Belief PA

MONTGOMERY

LIFE

DREAMSCAP

sweet dream

RECURRIN

hope